FIRST MARTYR

FIRST MARTYR

The Story of Saint Stephen

Nathan Michael Urban

Introduction

Whether Catholic or Protestant, every faithful Christian can agree that the saints lived extraordinary lives. Few of them, particularly those of the early Church, died peacefully (most of the Apostles of the first century died for their faith). Some, such as St. Peter, St. Vincent Ferrer, and St. Nicholas, were known for their ability to work miracles by the Divine Love, Grace, and Mercy of Jesus Christ. Others, such as St. Vincent de Paul, St. Damien de Veuster, St. Anthony of Padua, and St. Angela Merici to name a few among the many, have been remembered for their extreme generosity and sacrifice when serving the sick and destitute. Then of course there were the deep thinkers, fathers, or doctors of the Church. St. Paul, St. Ambrose, St. Jerome, St. Augustine, St. Pope Gregory the Great, and St. Thomas

Aquinas possessed not only some of the most profound and complex minds within the Catholic faith but within the scope of modern human history. Also among the saints were the great reformers of the Church such as St. Benedict, Pope St. Gregory the Great, St. Francis of Assisi, and St. Dominic, who brought about necessary change to Church doctrine, practices, and conduct in times of much needed reflection. Some, although not as many as other members of the Faith, served as popes. Pope Gregory the Great (there he is again), Pope Pius X, Pope Paul VI, and Pope John Paul II have all been canonized as saints in the Catholic Church. Yet still, a select group of saints never even walked the earth as humans. The archangels Michael, Gabriel, Raphael, and Uriel are all recognized saints in the Church.

Not every individual that has ever been canonized by the Holy Church sparks an immediate image or prayer associated with that particular saint (St. Ludger anyone?). The most revered of all the saints (and there are thousands of them and will continue to be more as long as the Holy Catholic Church is around) are the martyrs, those who defied their persecutors and died for the one

True Church. As stated earlier, nearly of the Apostles met their deaths as martyrs. St. Peter, the first pope of the Church (although he went by the title of Bishop of Rome), was notoriously crucified upside down during the reign of the monstrous Roman emperor Nero. During that same despot's reign St. Paul was beheaded, probably no later than A.D. 67. The lives of the other Apostles ended in similar brutal fashion. The deaths of some martyrs were so gruesome and inhumane (St. Lucy of Syracuse for example, whose eyes were gouged out after she'd refused to marry a pagan Roman), they are remembered merely for the horrific fates they suffered at the hands of their persecutors rather than any miraculous events or brilliant church reforms attributed to them. The macabre details of their deaths aside the martyrs, throughout the ages, have been venerated and remembered for their incredible courage, devout faith, and unwillingness to betray our Lord Jesus Christ when faced with torture and inevitable death. Like the agony, pain, and humility our Lord suffered during His Passion, the martyrs too were willing to leave their lives to the Divine Will of the Heavenly Father and bravely endure their last breaths with their faith fully intact. To paraphrase St. Paul, "I finished the race. I fought the good fight. I kept the faith."

Although St. John the Baptist was beheaded by order of the despicable king Herod Antipas and therefore, chronologically speaking, was martyred first, St. Stephen was the first martyr of the new Christian faith. He was the first person to die for his belief in and devotion to the New and Eternal Covenant promised and fulfilled by Our Lord Jesus Christ. Unfortunately, his death would not be the first and foreshadowed the many sufferings the members of the Catholic Christian faith would have to endure while under the rule of the mighty and altogether brutal hand of the very pagan Roman empire. In the pages to follow, the author attempts to capture not only the truth and essence of the young deacon's death but the timelessness of his sacrifice for a religion that always has been and always will be worth dying for.

Nathan Michael Urban

January 30, 2019

ONE

The Beginning of the New

The Galilean, Jesus of Nazareth, was dead. Tried, convicted, brutally flogged and beaten, he had died after several hours on the cross on Calvary just outside the walls of the holy city of Jerusalem. The tyrannical Roman governor of Judea, Pontius Pilate, along with the fanatical support of the Temple high priest Caiaphas and other members of the Sanhedrin, had sealed the fate of the troublesome prophet. Fearing for their lives, the remaining eleven of the disciples of the crucified Jesus went into hiding. The enemies of the man they had come to revere and accept as the Messiah had won. The holy Temple that Jesus had promised to destroy and rebuild in three days remained standing unscathed and unchanged. The movement, so exciting and full of promise at one point, was now over. Their master was dead and they would surely be next.

Or so everyone thought.

On that glorious Sunday morning, the third day of our Lord's death Mary Magdalene, accompanied by Joanna and Mary the mother of James, made their way to the tomb. Before they had reached their destination to mourn and pay their respects to the deceased teacher, healer, and prophet, they were stopped by an angel (most likely the archangel and our Heavenly Father's messenger, St. Gabriel) who informed them that the man they sought was no longer resting in his tomb. The angel declared that the crucified Jesus had been raised and that they were to go and see for themselves. "Do not be afraid! I know that you are seeking Jesus the crucified.

He is not here, for He has been raised just as He promised. Come and see the place where He lay." (Matthew 28: 5B-6)

No doubt astonished and perplexed by the angel's revelation, the women were then further instructed to go and tell the disciples once they had seen for themselves that the tomb of our Lord was indeed empty. After seeing that the stone that had once covered the tomb had been removed and that the Holy Shroud that had once concealed our Lord's crucified body no longer held His corpse, the three women left full of joy and fear to tell the eleven disciples the good news. However, while on their way to the find the disciples, the women were confronted by even greater revelation, one that surely put all their fears to rest. The risen Lord Jesus appeared to them in the flesh saying, "Peace! Do not be afraid! Go and carry the news to my brothers that they are to go to Galilee, where they will see me." (Matthew 28: 9-10)

Our Lord Jesus's resurrection had confirmed not only to the three women but eventually the eleven disciples and the rest of the world that the movement was not over. In fact, it had only just begun. The New and

Eternal Covenant was alive. Once in Galilee and in the presence of His disciples who saw our Lord and believed (Thomas took a little extra convincing and was only a believer in our Lord's resurrection after he'd touched the Son of Man's physical wounds of the crucifixion) Jesus declared: "All authority has been given to me in heaven and on earth. Therefore, go forth and teach all nations, baptizing them in the name of the Father and of the Son and of the Holy Spirit, teaching them to observe all that I have ever commanded you. And behold, I am with out always, even to the consummation of the age." (Matthew 28:20)

The story of the eleven disciples continued in the Book of Acts (also known as the Acts of the Apostles) where they went forth after being filled with the Holy Spirit (Acts 2:2-4) and did just as Jesus had commanded them by revealing the teachings of our Lord to Jews and Gentiles (non-Jews) alike. They converted many enduring both triumph and persecution. St. Peter (and later St. Paul after his conversion) led the way converting thousands of Jews and Gentiles. St. Paul's writings would end up as nearly half of what would eventually become the New Testament of the Holy Bible. Other notable Apostles of this most important period in the formation of the Church were Saints Luke, John the Evangelist, Timothy, Mark, James, and Barnabas. The men and women of this new and devout community lived simply as our Lord had during His time as a mortal on this earth. The Apostles traveled far encountering many different cultures in lands both foreign and ofttimes dangerous and hostile. According to some accounts, St. Thomas traveled as far as India where he was believed to have been beheaded by local radicals not receptive to the Word.

Resistance and persecution were always around the corner waiting like a ravenous beast ready to pounce upon its helpless prey. The Apostles, while certainly not helpless (St. Paul had been pretty handy with a sword in the first half of his life as Saul of Tarsus), were no doubt the target of the Jewish communities who refused to accept the teachings of the New Covenant preferring to continue with the old ways by observing Mosaic law. In their opinion, Jesus of Nazareth had not fulfilled all the promises of sacred scripture communicated through the prophets (Isaiah, Jeremiah, Daniel, etc.) in relation to the Messiah who would deliver Israel from the subjugation of its rulers (in this case, the Roman empire). Anyone who went against the teachings of the Old Covenant established by God through Moses was in effect committing an act of blasphemy and punishable by death.

The Gentile population, many of them pagan Romans and worshipers of such false gods as Jupiter, Saturn, and Mars, proved to be just as hostile towards the "Christ Jesus followers." After all, it had been the Romans who were ultimately responsible for our Lord's suffering and crucifixion. Rome and its numerous provinces had proven to be ruthless in the ability to rule over its subjects. Enslavement, imprisonment, heavy taxation, confiscation and destruction of property (not limited to only material goods and livestock but humans as well), and even death by beheading and crucifixion were just some of the ways the empire exacted tyranny over the inhabitants of its many conquered lands. In the minds of many loyal Romans, the early Christians were just one more group of people to conquer.

The task of subduing the members of the New Covenant, as both Jews and Gentiles (particularly those of Roman citizenship) soon found out, would not be so easily achieved. The followers of Jesus Christ, as they discovered, would preach the Truth even if it meant making the ultimate sacrifice of giving their very lives in the name of our Lord. One young man, a Greek-speaking Jew and Christian convert named Stephanos, would be the first give his life for the new and most Holy Church.

TWO

The Deacon and Apostle

There are several meanings of Stephanos or Stephen in the Greek language, the native tongue of our good saint. Translated as wreath, crown, reward, and honor, the two latter translations seem to exemplify the character, life, and death of the young martyr. For his faith in Christ, Stephen was rewarded a rightful place in Heaven. His death, though full of agony and pain, was at the same time courageous in his bearing witness to the teachings and Truth of our Lord Jesus.

The word *martyr*, an English word no doubt, is derived from its Greek equivalent (pronounced martyras in Greek) meaning "witness." As Christians and, more importantly as Catholic Christians, we are all called to bear witness to our Lord Jesus Christ. Unlike St. Stephen and the hundreds of martyrs that followed him, not all are called to shed their blood to the point of death. In this sense, martyrs are the highest of witnesses to our Lord because they made (and continue to make as in the case of the Christians in the Middle East currently being slaughtered for their faith by the hands of Islamic terrorists) the ultimate sacrifice.

Born around A.D. 5, Stephen and his family were most likely Hellenists, foreign-born Jews who spoke Greek. Hellenist converts like Stephen were minorities in the holy city of Jerusalem. While it is generally accepted that his Greek name was Stephanos, one little known tradition dating from the fifth century claimed that his original name was really Kelil, an Aramaic word meaning "crown." This is possible if Stephen was in fact born Jewish (there is little to no evidence that he was born a Gentile) for at least two reasons. First, Stephanos is the Greek equivalent of Kelil. Second, as evidenced by his lengthy speech in Acts 6 and 7, Stephen possessed a great knowledge of the history of Israel and Mosaic law. However, there is no evidence that he spoke Aramaic, the native tongue of our Lord and many other Jews from Galilee. Therefore, there is no reason for him to have been born with an Aramaic name since he and his family were Greek-speakers.

The origins of our saint's name aside, there are no details known about Stephen's childhood. What is known about him comes primarily from the Acts of the Apostles in chapters six and seven. The first mention of him is verse 5 of chapter 6 when he is appointed by the Apostles as one of seven deacons. In Greek, "diakonoi" is the equivalent of deacon. Its literal translation is "servant." Thus, Stephen was appointed by the Apostles, the first bishops of the Catholic Church, to be a servant of the Church and its parishioners. More specifically, the purpose of the original seven deacons was to care for the widows of the Greek-speaking population. Food distributions and other forms of care and hospitality were typically reserved first and foremost for the Hebrew-speaking widows since they were members of the majority population.

Tradition holds that Stephen was the oldest of the seven deacons and given the title of Archdeacon. Clearly, the deacons were all young men at the time of their appointment since Stephen himself had probably not yet reached the age of thirty in his new role. This is upheld by the fact that all art depicting the image of the saint reveals a youthful person. The Acts of the Apostles also seems to describe Stephen as having an angelic appearance. Verse 15 in chapter 6 states, "And all those sitting in the council, gazing at him, saw his face, as if it had become the face of an angel." Despite his age, Stephen seems to have possessed the knowledge, wisdom, and piety of an experienced and worldly soul. He is described in the Book of Acts as being full of the Holy Spirit and a great miracle worker. His teachings angered and aroused the suspicions of the synagogues. Naturally, they debated him but were unsuccessful in their attempts to silence him.

There is also no reason to believe that Stephen did not approach his duties as a deacon very seriously when caring for the poor widows of Jerusalem. Whenever possible, he evangelized them with the teachings of Christ. Tragically, his time as a servant of the Church and teacher of the revelations of our Lord Jesus would be very short-lived. It was his knowledge, piety, and passion for the Truth that would soon draw the ire of the Sanhedrin bringing about one of the most remarkable and fiery defenses of our Catholic faith to be found within the pages of the New Testament.

THREE

Speech to the Sanhedrin

According to Acts, Stephen's teachings in the synagogues angered many of the members. Charged with blasphemy for preaching against Mosaic law, he was taken away and brought to the Sanhedrin to be judged for his alleged crimes. Once in the presence of his earthly judges, Stephen offered an emotional and blistering defense for his teaching of the Truth.

The speech of Stephen the Archdeacon to the Sanhedrin was, at its core, a presentation of the history of Israel and how the teachings of Jesus Christ, the risen Savior and the Messiah promised to the world by the prophets of the Old Testament, had fulfilled rather than subverted the laws of Moses. By approaching the Sanhedrin, the devout body of Temple priests who oversaw and interpreted Mosaic law, with such an argument reveals the courageous and faith-driven character of Stephen. It had only been a few short years since the same Sanhedrin (although probably not all the same priests) had interrogated and charged our Lord with the crime of blasphemy for declaring Himself the Son of God. The task of convincing these men of the old way that their laws were no longer viable in a world where all the prophecies of the coming Messiah had been fulfilled in the person of Jesus of Nazareth would prove to be one debate that young archdeacon would not win.

Nevertheless, what would end up as the longest of all the speeches given by the Apostles in the Book of Acts (it comprises nearly all of chapter seven) served as not only a thorough and passionate defense of the our

Lord's role as the promised Messiah but also an indictment to accept anything that did not fit into their narrow perspective of sacred scripture. At one point in his speech, Stephen goes as far to call the Sanhedrin "stiff-necked" and resisting the Holy Spirit just as their ancestors had done before them. In Acts 7:51-53, Stephen is quoted as saying, "Was there ever a prophet your ancestors did not persecute? They even killed those who predicted the coming of the Righteous One (Jesus of Nazareth). And now you have betrayed and murdered Him."

The prophets Stephen referred to in his speech were possibly Isaiah and Jeremiah since both men, particularly Isaiah, had predicted the coming of our Savior. Both men did suffer persecution during their lifetime. The Talmud, the book of Jewish law, even states that Isaiah was martyred. However, the nature of Isaiah's death is not revealed in the Bible. If he is in fact one of the prophets mentioned by Stephen in the passage from Acts 7, then this is further proof that Stephen was in fact raised Jewish. Prior to the Talmud being officially written down in the fourteenth century, everything in

Jewish law was passed down orally. This of course is true of the Bible as well since Tradition always predated Holy Scripture.

Stephen continues his indictment of the Sanhedrin in Acts chapter 7, verse 48. The building of the Temple, in his point of view, was an act of idolatry much like in the vein of Aaron's golden calf from the Book of Exodus. "The Most High does not dwell in houses made with hands." Simply put our Lord, omnipotent in every way, is everywhere. Although he was correct to point out such a contradiction in the belief of an all-powerful being, Stephen's opinion of Temple worship was, even for his time, one held to be more negative than those of his fellow Apostles and early Christians.

For many Jews and even early Christian converts, the Temple was the holiest and most sacred of all places. Saint Paul, one of Stephen's persecutors, still visited the Temple after his miraculous conversion. One possible reason for converts such as St. Paul in refusing to give up regular visitations to the Temple may lie in an applied significance to the sacrificial rites practiced within its walls. It is likely some early Christians may have continued to frequent the Temple in order to help form the theological interpretation of our Lord's sacrifice on the Cross. Others perhaps were simply unwilling to completely abandon the rituals of their former faith. Whatever the reasons, Stephen did not appear to have shared either sentiment when it came to the old ways of Temple worship.

The conclusion of Stephen's speech is arguably the most powerful moment in his defense of his faith for he goes as far to condemn the Sanhedrin and their ancestors for not keeping the laws given to them by God. In Acts 7:53, he says, "You received the law by the actions of Angels, and yet you have not kept it." The reaction of the Sanhedrin upon hearing this very hard but altogether proven truth was to gnash their teeth in bitter anger. But Stephen does not relent at this point. He all buts seals his fate with his words in verse 55. "Behold, I see the heavens opened, and the Son of Man standing at the right hand of God."

The Sanhedrin had heard enough.

FOUR

The Death of Stephen

Seething with a vengeful anger, the Sanhedrin had Stephen removed from their court and dragged to a location beyond the city walls of Jerusalem. Exactly where Stephen was brought to be executed by stoning for blasphemy is still unknown. Tradition provides us with two separate accounts as to where the saint's execution took place. One account holds that he was martyred just beyond the northern gate of the city while the second suggests that he was felled near the eastern gate.

The same uncertainty can be said of the exact year of Stephen's death. Scholars typically put the year of his martyrdom between A.D. 34 and A.D. 36, making the deacon around the age of thirty when he met his agonizing fate. It is also unclear as to the exact role Saul of Tarsus, a Pharisee and zealot who would later be reborn as the great Apostle and Church father Saint Paul, played in the death of Stephen.

What is certain is that Stephen, filled with the Holy Spirit and the love of our Lord Jesus, met his end with the courage, humility, and peace reserved only for the martyrs of our True Faith. As the first martyr (protomartyr some call him), his death would become the example for all those who gave their very last breath for the Faith, including St. Paul.

Among the Jewish populations of ancient Judea and Galilee, death by stoning was the most common as well as, arguably, the most brutal form of capital punishment. It was our Lord who saved another saint, Mary Magdalene, from this violent fate in the Gospel of

John, chapter 8, verse 7. For the sin of adultery, the scribes and Pharisees had condemned her to death. But our Lord, always the wisest among His fellow men, stated, "Let whoever is without sin among you be the first to cast a stone at her." It was our Lord's mercy that saved this woman from certain death and at the same time instilled, at least momentarily, a degree of humility and self-reflection among her would-be executioners.

Paralleling our Lord Jesus's mercy in the Gospel of John, Stephen too showed profound mercy when facing his executioners. As the stones pounded his mortal body inflicting extreme pain while the moment of death crept ever so closer with each new wound Stephen, rather than condemn his persecutors for their murderous hatred, asked our Lord to forgive them. In Acts 7:59 Stephen, after having asked the Lord Jesus to receive his spirit and falling to his knees, cried out to our Lord and said, "Lord, do not hold this sin against them." These were the final words of Stephen who, bloodied and on his knees, had called out to the Lord Jesus for forgiveness for the sins of his murderers.

Perhaps an even more direct parallel between the mercy shown by Stephen in the moments before his death and that of our Lord Jesus can be found in the Gospel of Luke. In Chapter 23, verse 34, our Lord, while hanging from the Cross on Calvary, looked up to His Father in Heaven and said, "Father, forgive them. For they know not what they do." Our Lord Jesus was, of course, referring to his those in the crowd who mocked him and the Roman executioners nearby. The point of Stephen's words and actions in the face of impending death could be that he was a man of unbreakable faith and one who truly walked in the image of Christ. How wonderful for the one who is the first martyr of the True Faith.

FIVE

The Aftermath and the Role of Saul of Tarsus

Stephen was dead. The same fate he had accused the Sanhedrin of instilling on the prophets before him had befallen him. The shock of his sudden and violent death caused the remaining Apostles in Jerusalem to flee to other cities many settling in Antioch, an ancient Greek city in modern-day Turkey that would become one of the major bases of the early Catholic Church.

Prior to the voluntary exile of the Apostles, some of them gathered the battered body of Stephen and buried him in an unknown location. According to Acts 8:2, "Godly men buried Stephen and mourned for him." The Godly men of course were his fellow Apostles although exactly which ones is not known.

Another aspect of Stephen's martyrdom is the degree of involvement carried out by Saul of Tarsus. At the very least, it is known and accepted by every scholar and Christian theologian that he was a witness to Stephen's death. What is still being debated to this day is whether or not Saul was an active participant. The Orthodox Church believes that Saul only kept watch of the garments of the Sanhedrin who stoned Stephen. The Aramaic Bible however states that he physically held the garments during while the Apostle was being murdered. This is in fact confirmed in Acts 22 when Saul, now Paul, recounts his conversion to the True Faith. Confessing to our Lord Jesus in verse 20, Paul says, "And when the blood of Your witness Stephen was poured out, I stood nearby and was consenting, and I watched over the garments of those who put him to death."

Paul admits to being "consenting" to the sentence passed and carried out on Stephen. In other words, he approved of the public execution of a man whose only crime was professing the Truth about our Lord Jesus Christ. The event seems to have had a very profound and lasting effect on Paul. In 1 Timothy 1:12-13, Paul says, "I give thanks to Him who had strengthened me, Christ Jesus our Lord, because He has considered me faithful, placing me in the ministry, though previously I was a blasphemer, and a persecutor, and contemptuous. But then I obtained the mercy of God. For I had been acting ignorantly, in unbelief." The anointed Apostle of Christ goes on to say in chapter 15, "It is a faithful saying, and worthy of acceptance by everyone, that Christ Jesus came into this world to bring salvation to sinners, among whom I am first."

Even though he never directly mentions Stephen in the above passages, St. Paul clearly felt immense guilt over his time spent as a persecutor of Christians before his conversion during that fateful journey to Damascus. "Among whom I am first," he'd said. "First" meaning the worst kind of sinner. It is reasonable to believe that

St. Paul carried the death of Stephen with him up until the moment of his own martyrdom around the year A.D. 67. Our Lord Jesus had forgiven him for his sins and crimes but St. Paul, a man wracked with guilt throughout the second half of his life, had possibly never forgiven himself.

SIX

Saint Stephen In History

As is the case with all the great saints and martyrs of the Holy Catholic Church, their stories did not end with their deaths or canonizations. Tales connected to them and their glory as servants of our Lord Jesus Christ and His Holy Church have stretched across two millennia. Stories connected to life and death of St. Stephen are, like many other tales of Catholic Christian saints, the products of confirmed facts and profound legends.

Perhaps the first recorded story about Stephen concerned the location of his burial. In the year A.D.

415, a Catholic priest named Lucian had a dream in which the location of Stephen's burial was revealed to him. In the dream, Lucian saw the tomb of St. Stephen in a monastery named Beit Jamal. It was in a cave near the site that the remains of the saint were supposed to have been laid to rest. Today, Beit Jimal stands near the Israeli town of Beit Shemesh and is run by Salesian monks. The site continues to be honored as a possible site that once held the remains of the Blessed martyr.

In that same year of A.D. 415 on December 26th, relics believed to be those of Stephen were taken the Church of Hagia Sion, a Byzantine basilica in the holy city of Jerusalem. Since the actual date of his martyrdom was not known (and still isn't as of this writing), the day of December 26th was established as the Feast Day of Saint Stephen. The church was destroyed in a siege in A.D. 614 but later reconstructed in the 12th century and renamed the Abbey of the Dormition of the Virgin Mary. Since 1998, the Abbey of the Dormition of the Virgin Mary has been known as the Hagia Maria Sion Abbey in honor of the original church and is run by Benedictine monks.

The relics from the Church of Hagia Sion were transferred in the year A.D. 439 to newly constructed church built north of the Damascus Gate. The Byzantine empress Aelia Eudocia, wife of emperor Theodosius II, herself a devout Christian and inspired by a pilgrimage to Jerusalem, had ordered the building of the church in honor of St. Stephen. As with the Church of Hagia Sion, it met the same fate when it was destroyed in the 12th century but later rebuilt. Today it stands as St. Stephen's Basilica in Jerusalem and is also known by its French name, Saint Etienne.

Saint Stephen has even found a place among Crusader lore. The Crusaders, the great defenders of the Holy Catholic Church and Christian pilgrims between the 11th and 15th centuries, had named the northern gate of Jerusalem as "Saint Stephen's Gate." The name remained in place until after the destruction of the Hagia Sion. Muslim rulers in the city prohibited any Christians from approaching the northern city wall. To settle the conflict, the name of Saint Stephen's Gate was transferred to the eastern gate of the city where to this day it is still known by that name honoring the great martyr.

SEVEN

The Legacy of St. Stephen

The final legacy of St. Stephen, the protomartyr, is one identical with every man or woman that has been canonized a saint in the Holy Catholic Church. Through their sainthood and their patronage, the lives of these great men and women live on through prayer and veneration. Some, like the subject of this little book, have been gone (physically speaking) for nearly two millennia. Yet, because of their high place in the Church as true servants of the Heavenly Father, their names and the extraordinary events that made them worthy of canonization and continued veneration remind us that our lives are never in lived in vain long as we fully embrace our purpose as followers of the one True Faith. For the saints, and hopefully for every Christian, that purpose is to live the teachings of our Lord Jesus Christ all the days of our relatively short time in this world.

Saint Stephen most certainly lived the teachings of Our Lord.

In addition to the Holy Catholic Church, Stephen is venerated as a saint in the Lutheran, Anglican, Oriental Orthodox, and Eastern Orthodox churches. The events, deeds, and personalities of the saints have always determined the patronages designated to their names. The first archdeacon, servant of the poor and miracle worker, Stephen was martyred through death by stoning. Therefore, he is the patron saint of altar servers, deacons, masons, headaches. He is also the patron saint of horses. Additionally, Stephen is the patron saint of Toulouse, France, the Diocese of Metz (France), and the Diocese of Owensboro in the state of Kentucky.

Every known depiction of Stephen, whether in stained-glass or a canvas painting, pictures him as being youthful and often carrying three stones, a Gospel book, and a miniature church. He is typically shown wearing the traditional robes of a deacon while carrying a palm, the symbol of martyrdom. While the appearance of a palm is certainly justified given the saint's violent and significant death, the deacon robes represent attire that had not yet been established during Stephen's lifetime. Deacon robes were not invented and instituted as standard garments until centuries after his martyrdom. Another discrepancy worth noting are the Eastern Orthodox depictions commonly showing the saint swinging a censer of blessed incense, a practice more frequently used in the Orthodox church.

The holy relics of the saints are for many Catholics priceless treasures to be cherished and venerated. They provide not only a physical connection to the saints (especially if they are first-class relics meaning the items were once personally owned or physical parts of the saints) but a profoundly spiritual one as well. Some, like the Holy Shroud of Turin and fragments of the True Cross, even have a direct connection to our good Lord Himself. However, as is the case of such highly venerated and early saints as Saint Joseph and many of the Apostles, there exists no known physical relics with direct ties to the lives and deaths of these holy men and women.

The relics of Saint Stephen exist purely in the tales of legends rather than confirmed, documented facts. One popular legend is most definitely an invention of the 9th century. The Imperial Regalia of the Holy Roman Empire includes a relic known as St. Stephen's Purse. It is an elaborate gold and jewel-covered box believed to contain soil soaked with the blood of the protomartyr. Another supposed first-class relic of the saint is part of his right arm that is enshrined in the Trinity Lavra of St. Sergius in present-day Russia. Perhaps the only credible account of any relics actually existing or having once existed can be found in *The City of God*, the timeless work by the great Church Doctor, Saint Augustine of Hippo. Within the pages of this powerful 5th century defense of Christianity, Saint Augustine describes accounts of several miracles attributed to Saint Stephen when parts of his relics were brought to Africa. Given Saint Augustine's impeccable reputation for piety and honesty, it is very unlikely that his chronicles of these events are a fabrication.

Beyond great theological works like the ones of St. Augustine, Stephen has also found a place in song and the Christmas season. One of the oldest and most revered Christmas carols of all-time, "Good King Wenceslas" tells the story of King Wenceslas (actually a 10th century Bohemian duke who was martyred and later canonized a saint in the Catholic Church) and his journey to deliver alms to the poor on a very snowy and stormy night on the Feast of St. Stephen, December the 26th or the second day the Christmas season. While not as commonly heard today, the carol was especially popular in Great Britain for many years.

In countries that have been traditionally Catholic, Anglican, or Lutheran, St. Stephen's Day (or the Feast of St. Stephen) is still a public holiday. In the Eastern and Oriental Orthodox churches (Coptic, Syrian, and Malankara), the saint's feast day is celebrated a day later, on the 27th of December. This is due to the fact that the Orthodox churches follow the modified Julian calendar rather than the more Westernized Gregorian calendar followed by the Catholic, Anglican, and Lutheran churches. The Russian Orthodox church, which uses the traditional Julian calendar, observes the Feast of St. Stephen on January 9th, the third day of their Nativity celebration.

EIGHT

Prayers

This little book would not be complete without a couple of the most commonly said prayers to the great protomartyr. Through the intercession of Saint Stephen, we pray that the Heavenly Father will bless us with the same courage, strength, love, and devotion to the Lord Jesus that our good saint possessed up until the last breath of his short life. We also hope, that in praying for the saint's intercession, that our faith in the Lord Jesus Christ will never waiver even in the most trying and desperate of times.

A Prayer by Deacon Keith Fournier

Lord Jesus, You chose Stephen as the first deacon and martyr of Your one,

Holy, Catholic and Apostolic Church.

The heroic witness of his holy life and death

reveals Your continued presence among us.

Through following the example of his living faith,

and by his intercession, empower us by Your Holy Spirit

to live as witnesses to the faith in this New Missionary Age.

No matter what our state in life,

career or vocation,

help us to proclaim, in both word and deed,

the fullness of the Gospel to a world which is waiting

to be born anew in Jesus Christ.

Pour out upon Your whole Church,

the same Holy Spirit which animated St. Stephen,
Martyr,

to be faithful to the end,

which is the beginning of the life eternal in the
communion of the Trinity. Amen.

St. Stephen

O Glorious St. Stephen, first of the martyrs,

for the sake of Christ you gave up your life

in testimony of the truth of His divine teaching.

Obtain for us, dear St. Stephen, the faith, the
hope,

the love, and the courage of martyrs.

When we are tempted to shirk our duty

or deny our faith, come to our assistance

as a shining example of the courage of martyrs,

and win for us a love like your own.

We ask it of you for the honor of Jesus Christ, our
Lord

who is the model and reward of all martyrs. Amen.

Made in the USA
Monee, IL
17 June 2021

71601639R00028